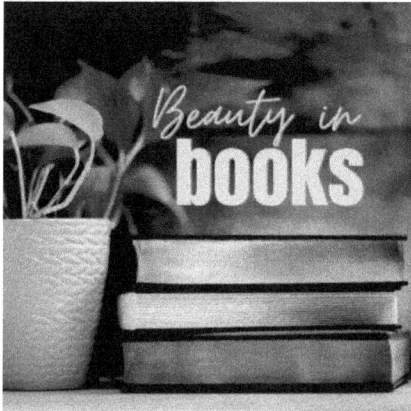

About the Author

"Abyy Sparklewood is an accomplished author with a unique talent for crafting captivating children's fiction and insightful business books. With a playful imagination and a keen business sense, her stories ignite young minds and inspire entrepreneurs to reach new heights of success."

AUTUMNS PALETTE
COLORING THE BEAUTY OF AUTUMN

FALL FLOWERS

Autumn
Reading Nook

Cornucopia

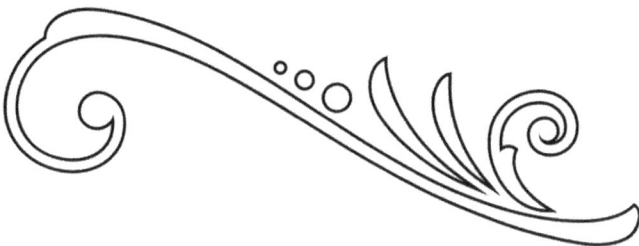
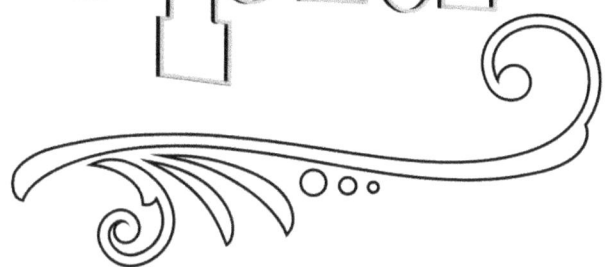

FOREST FRIENDS

APPLE ORCHARD

Fall Fair

BONFIRE NIGHT

CIDER MILL

ACORN ADVENTURES

Hayride Excursion

CRISP AUTUMN MORNING

HAUNTED HOUSE

CIDER MILL

Maple Syrup Harvest

GINGERBREAD HOUSE

FOREST FRIENDS

MUSHROOMS

CABIN IN THE WOODS

Today will be a gREAT Day

BE positive

BE POSITIVE ALWAYS

FALL LEAVES

FOREST MAGIC

Check out my other books by
Scanning the QR code or using
the link below

linktr.ee/beautyinbooks3